CW01072531

SUNSHINE IN THE WEEDS

D.A. IRSIK

SUNSHINE IN THE WEEDS

by D. A. Irsik

Anamcara Press LLC

Published in 2024 by Anamcara Press LLC

Author © 2024 Debra Irsik

Cover art by Glendora Paxton, (reference photo from Palette Knife Painting Techniques.) http://www.youtube.com/channel/@paletteknifepaintingtutori6038.

Interior art by Staci Hammon

Book design by Maureen Carroll

Perpetua and Minion Pro.

Printed in the United States of America.

Book Description: A collection of poems.

ANAMCARA PRESS LLC

P.O. Box 442072, Lawrence, KS 66044

https://anamcara-press.com/

Ordering Information:

Quantity sales. Special discounts are available on quantity purchases by corporations, associations, and others. For details, contact the publisher at the address above.

Orders by U.S. trade bookstores and wholesalers. Please contact Ingram Distribution.

Irsik, Debra, Author, Sunshine in the Weeds

POE023030/Animals and Nature

POE023010/Grief/loss

POE023050/Family

POE003000/Inspirational;Religious

ISBN-13: 978-1-960462-40-4 (Paperback)

ISBN-13: 978-1-960462-41-1 (Hardcover)

Library of Congress Control Number: 2024933963

Contents

PART III: Seasons and Nature

ALSO BY D. A. IRSIK:

The Heroes by Design series for upper Middle Grade:

Heroes by Design book 1: published in 2020
Hero's Journey book 2: published in 2020
Hero's Purpose book 3: published in 2021

Irsik also contributed to the following journals:

105 Meadowlark Reader/Bicycle issue 3/Spring 2022/(*Blue English Racer.*) and Food/issue 4/Fall/2022/(*Little Things.*)
The Write Bridge, Summer 2023 edition: *Perilous and Playful*

DEDICATION:
This collection is dedicated the fifteen-year-old me.
The me who doubted possibility.

INTRODUCTION

MY POETRY

It's not high brow
tea party fare.
You won't find
my poetry there.

It's poetry about
your life and mine.
About love, nature,
moments, and time.

It's like folk music.
Stories simple and true.
Memories we share.
Snapshots of life for you.

No, this is not
that poetry you hate.
The essence is there,
but it's changed of late.

Written in language
you'll understand,
and if there's no rhyme
there's no reprimand.

My poetry is about
our sorrow and strife,
love and joy,
faith and life.

PART I:
MEMORIES & REFLECTION

Take time to make memories;
they are the treasure
you leave behind.

HOME

Home is where
We are happy
With people we love
And foods that comfort
It is that ornery gleam in
Grandma's eye

Home is not a place
It is a warm embrace
A smile from a sister or brother
There is no pretense
No posing
You are who you are

Home is not a faraway place
Not a house
Not a town
It is any place
Your heart is known
Where love is unconditional

Your childhood home
Is just a house
Until filled with loved ones
Sharing memories
Laughing … loving … caring
That's home

Debra Irsik

GRANDMA'S HOUSE

Memories stir as I drive by
Grandma's buff colored stucco house.
Most of my early years
unfolded between those walls.
Playing paper-dolls;
making Kleenex angels
endless hours watching
my brother's train go
round and round, changing tracks.
We tried to get it to hold our Barbies
as they traveled between imaginary towns.
We played dress up in the backyard,
had cook-outs and ran with cousins;
carving our names in the old oak tree,
or swinging in the tire.
We tried to rescue baby birds,
begging Grandma for milk
to put in doll bottles.
She nodded her head and let
us learn our lessons
of life and death.
We rode bikes and
rolled in the fall leaves that
smelled of dirt and sun.
We danced in the rain;
became pirates and princesses,
cowboys and Indians.
Such were the happy days of childhood.

OAK OR ELM

Buff-colored suede stucco,
that was Grandma's house.
A peeling white picket fence
on one side of the backyard,
a copycat garage
on the other.
Further back by the alley
was an incinerator.
We broke up limbs and shoveled
fall leaves into its hungry top.
It belched earthy white smoke.

There was a lone tree in the backyard.
I thought it an oak
from fairytales and dreams,
but it might have been an elm.
Grandpa hung a tire swing
from a sturdy limb.
We took turns swinging
with endlessly pumping legs.

I meant for my initials
to be carved in that tree,
but

Debra Irsik

fate intervened.
My brother carved his
first true love's initials
on the tree with his own.
Then he dropped the pocketknife
where it found its mark
on my waiting forehead below.
The only remembrance of
my first loves initials
is the scar I carry
above my left brow.

GOLDIE

We hopscotched, skipped, and walked home
to grandma's house. My brother stopped.
Crouching on the broken concrete sidewalk,
he put out his hands and made kissing noises
to a frightened puppy.
It wagged and whined and licked.
So, he picked it up.
My two sisters and I shook our heads.
I said,
"Grandma won't let you keep it."
He shrugged, "She might."
I nodded with the wisdom
of an eight-year-old.
"She won't. You're just going
to make it harder by bringing it home."
My sisters and I exchanged a knowing look.

My brother held an extra-special place
in Grandma's heart.
The first grandson place.
He begged and tried to make the
puppy do tricks to show Grandma
how smart it was.
Unsurprisingly, Grandma caved.
"With one condition,
we will put an ad in the paper."
LOST PUPPY.
The day the paper came out
we rushed home
breathless with fear;

7

someone might have called.
We said our silent, collective prayers,
that the puppy was dumped, not lost.
By the end of the week
no one had called.
So,
Goldie, (she was a golden cocker spaniel)
was now a member of our family.
Our companion and friend.
Four wounded children
and
one found puppy.

GRANNY

Her hair, braided; twisted in a bun.
She is short of stature,
but of heart,
the biggest one.

Growing up, we measure,
soon we can look down,
upon the head we treasure,
but she still wears the crown.

She's proud to be an American.
Her in-laws could attest.
When they talk to us in German,
she says, "English is best."

She loves to go fishing,
off the bank of the pond,
with her handy cane pole,
and red bandana on.

If you can't find her
I would propose,
she'll be bent in the garden
nurturing a rose.

She's a little German whirlwind.
Her flowers delight so many,
and she receives her mail
addressed simply, *Granny*.

Debra Irsik

YOU TAUGHT

Outwardly you fit the description of an old maid schoolteacher,
your short silver waves, mid-calf straight skirts and cardigans;
no-nonsense, straight-forward look and military posture.
We could have been fooled; others were.

I came to you all doodles and daydreams,
taking advantage of my disadvantage.
Poor little girl from a broken home.
You smiled, and it reached your eyes.

You Taught
by reading to us,
Uncle Tom's Cabin, by Harriet Beecher Stowe;
the horror of hate and prejudice.
One woman who initiated
change in a nation with only her pen.

You Taught
that we are never too old to believe
in Santa Claus.
Challenging us to figure out
why you still believed,
eyes twinkling like a child.
You showed us the spirit of giving
is Santa Claus.
With our tumbleweed Christmas tree
and in our newfound understanding,
we believed.

You Taught
Consequences.
Whether the best student or the worst
it made no difference.
If eyes wandered during a spelling test
you presented the culprit with an outstretched hand,
and crumpled the offending paper in front of the class;
file 13, no excuses.

You Taught
memorization of math facts.
The dreaded time tests at your desk.
Hoping to get a star.
I realize now how much we learned.

You Taught,
that a single woman
could raise an adopted son,
standing against the tide.
You stood for: courage, honor,
discipline and respect.

Thank you for teaching.

FOREVER A MEMORY

Graduation
An ending
A beginning
New experiences
Friendship's loom
Relationships
Forged for twelve-years
Soon connected by a thread
Life is a collage
Of collected moments
Friendships that weather
Distance and time
Should be treasured
But
We didn't know
Those early friendships
Would set a precedent
For future relationships
Some recognized
As shallow and self-serving
Some worthy of more
Than we gave

We hear the warning
In your lifetime, you will
Have one or two genuine friends
We don't grasp its meaning
Until we live life
It's that connection
With the friend you might see
Every few years

And pick up right
Where you left off
Sharing secrets-joys-sorrows
Disappointments-love
Accomplishments and victories
Knowing only they
Would understand
I wish I had nurtured that friendship
Held it in higher esteem
I should have been
More present in her life
Celebrating her moments
Before she became
Forever a memory

JACKIE

When I think of you, I see a blue Mustang,
your ready smile, with a sprinkle of freckles.
Going back to the first time, the school bell rang.
Our fifth-grade year, of pony-tails, boys, and giggles.

We shared forty-fives, dancing to the Beatles;
whispering our deepest, darkest secrets.
Lives intertwined like sewing stitches,
sharing our hopes, our dreams, our deepest regrets.

The gaited Pomp and Circumstance stepped.
You to be a nurse, me in beauty school.
Marriage and family, the distance crept,
our words sprinkled in cards and baby drool.

Though tested and battered,
your body crippled by pain,
you always did what mattered;
Lifting others again and again.

WISH I WAS FISHIN'

Sit'n on the dock on a hot July day.
Wish'n I had a pole.
Listening to the Ol' Cottonwood
laughing at me.

Wind pushing little ripples,
under my feet.
Fish merrily flipping by,
not even a hook on a stick
to tease them with.

No minnow or nightcrawler
to tantalize.
Just Kansas wind,
an old farm girl,
and memories sweeping by.

Gnarly roots seek the cool water.
The tree leans precariously
over the shimmering green pool.
Moss clinging to the edges.
Little tadpoles dart in and out,
like children playing tag at recess.

A chain clanks on an old shed,
adding to the song of the meadowlark and dove.
As shadows fall, frogs and toads
lend their baritone and bass.
A symphony heard only when
quietly, we take a breath.
Listen.

BARBECUE

Chinese lanterns sway
to the dancing of their feet.
They laugh, sing, and play,
sawing fiddles keep the beat.
Children sing in rhyme,
tapping their toes a little.
Everyone keeping time
to melodies of the fiddle.

The fire's roaring.
It crackles and pops.
Young hearts soaring.
The music never stops.

Images bending in the flame,
a mirage of laughing faces.
Lightening threatens rain.
The whole gang races.

Under the tents cover,
old men are telling tales.
Wagging tongues hover,
and the fiddlers' music sails.

EXCERPT FROM LIFE I

I remember listening to the rain as a child and thinking that it was God's tears. I pictured this gentle, white-bearded man crying, because the people He loved so dearly were so mixed up and sinful. Not wanting to contribute to God's sadness, I made up my mind to always be good. I would be the one that did not distress God.

Soon enough, I learned that we all sin, and no matter how hard we try, we still sometimes screw up. I also learned that God still loved me. I have been angry and disappointed in something my children have done, but no matter what, I still love them. We are taught that God's love is so much bigger than that. We cannot understand the love He has for us. It is beyond comprehension.

I admit, doubt creeps in when life gets hard. Annie's birthmarks. John's disability, family and relationships all caused me to question. Annie's death caused me to doubt my faith and the very existence of God. Those were the darkest days of my life.

I have decided, life happens and it is how we choose to deal with it that makes God an integral part of it. Sometimes we make choices that ease our burdens in life, and sometimes we add to those burdens. We have to ask God to forgive us, and help us bear the consequences of those decisions.

I do not believe we are all created equal. Some have a lot more going for them from the start. I do believe that each of us has something to contribute to the world around us, whether or not we are in ideal circumstances. Usually those who have to go the greatest distance are the best kind of people. I wish those with the disadvantages could know that their contributions are just as important as anyone elses. God sees us. He knows our hearts, and He has created a place for us.

Debra Irsik

PAULINE

Crepe paper skin
Vacant blind eyes
Rambling words strung
Into memorized verses
Words mined from memory
To remind us of who
She once was
She is not needy or unhappy
Not bored or lonely
Not today
Today she is glad
Glad we are here
She is anxious to spend time
Time of which
She is filled to the brim
Time which she has the luxury
To waste without care
Tomorrow may or
May not come
She gives us precious
Golden nuggets freely
She does not hold back
Offering all she has
All that is left of importance
Is contained in this vessel
And she may or may not recall
Your name or relationship

Her stories are repeated
Moments lost
Regained
Memories made
To pass to those who take
  Time to touch
  To learn
 To listen
To cherished words
Precious moments
That would otherwise
Be lost like morning fog

Debra Irsik

A LIFE LIVED WELL

What signifies a life lived well
After all these years who can tell

Hard work and play
  Put others first
    Those were the things
      We learned in verse
Be a role model
  Generosity
    Love
      Empathy
Keep values in place
  Understanding
    Kindness
      And Grace
Learn from mistakes
  Begin everyday new
    Find purpose in difficulty
      Always be true
Provide peace
  Avoid confrontation
    Be honorable
      Show appreciation
Make the most of the gifts
  Given to you
    Let Christ lead
      Love as He loves you

EVIDENCE OF JOY

Lips together
thin rose line
one corner slightly lifts
the other concedes
A smile
But
Eyebrows lift
Eyes open wide and bright
drawing in those around
to share a moment
THAT
Is
JOY

Debra Irsik

REFLECTION

Image
Mirror
Distorted
Unreal
Untrue
Surface
Past can be a reflection of the future.
Can I shape it?
What is my part in the plan?
I quiet my voice to hear
You whisper the truth.
Open my eyes to see
The real me;
Erase the distorted version I see.
In my reflection.

WHO AM I?

I will never stand before a

Roaring crowd and receive a Nobel Prize.

I will not be on the podium with that humble smile,

Or confident presence raising my arms in victory.

Clasping my chest with humble thanks.

I will be the cheerleader in the crowd;

The worker bee in the background,

Clapping, whistling, and cheering

With tears of joy running down

My face as

My child,

My mentor, my friend,

Receives the accolades.

I will have the satisfaction

Of knowing that, I made

A difference even if I don't

Wear the crown.

LOVE

Love is always
Given with the hope that it's returned
Sometimes overrated justly
But often anticipated
With a fluttering of hearts

UNCONDITIONAL LOVE

Child
Joy
Precious
Heartfelt tears
Overflowing with
Irrational hormonal highs
The wonder of total
Unconditional love

THE WOMAN THAT I AM

Mom
Martyr
Sister
Daughter
Wife
Christian.
But who
Listens?

Everything
To Everyone
But
Me.

Is it selfish,
Not earned,
Narcissistic
But learned?

If I don't
Take a stand
Make a fuss
Raise my hand.

I know
I will fade
From the woman
I am.

TIMELINE OF LIFE

Timeline of life,
What would it read?
Birth
Life
Death
Anything in-between?
Is there more?
What was this life for?
Joy
Pain
Tears
Spinning through years.
A flipbook picture show.
What purpose?
One life touched
One heart moved
One soul saved
What is your
Timeline of life?

PART II:
LIFE LESSONS

Life is your teacher, take notes.

MORE THAN WE NEED

What do we gain, striving for more than we need?
Doesn't that encourage lust for power and greed?
Should a man work to be at the top of the heap?
Or will that dig him in too deep?

God promised abundance to His people of praise.
But we left out one inadmissible phrase.
It's taking these gifts with no recognition.
To claim the feat with selfish permission.

It's simple really, all He asks.
Is to give Him the glory in those tasks.
When you reap more than you need,
give to another and plant a seed.

Share your bounty with a sister or brother.
Take care of one another.
Give thanks when your ship comes in,
and turn away from greed and sin.

Our lives are meant to be full,
And we're expected to turn from Satan's pull.
The thirst for power is overwhelming and strong,
but power without love is incredibly wrong.

HEROINES

My heroines were
sweet, faithful,
naïve and strong.
Saving the day with
sweet nature and kindness,
morality, and faith.

Anne, mischievous, inquisitive,
and hopeful.

Pollyanna, deeply rooted in faith
and positivity.
Sometimes naivety protected her from
life's cruel moments.

Heidi, sweet, loving and open.
She was kind, conscientious, and
willing to give of herself.

"Uncle Tom's Cabin," helped to
instill in me a sense of fairness
and acceptance of all.

"Little Women," and
"Pride and Prejudice,"

with their powerful characters
and substance,
helped me find my balance
in faith, empathy, and
the desire to be a giver.
These heroines had one thing
in common.
They each had
Heart.

Debra Irsik

OUR REALITY

Yesterday's fiction becomes our reality.
Today's fantasy is a frightening possibility.
News is propaganda; truth is only as good
as the person speaking.

Words stretched to extremes,
slanted to the speaker's preference.
Fake is a buzzword:
fake news, fake web sites.
Companies, phone solicitations,
all fake, with the intention to take.
Take from you, from me, from humanity.

Truth has become relative to a plan,
or a goal to boost an individual agenda.
Self-serving and totally acceptable,
as long as it furthers the cause.

Should we be wary of today's truth?
Guard against the pull of the tide?
Find our truth deep inside?
Stand firm in a world that is shapeshifting,
becoming a boomerang of
Words
Actions
That can fly back at us.

A BLANK SCREEN

Standing in a meadow
before a blank screen,
she wonders,
what her movie will be?

She lifts her face to the heavens,
raising her arms and turning slowly.
The wind comes swirling around her.
Tears stream down her cheeks.

As the wind grows stronger,
her hair whips her face.
She's pushed back, losing her balance.
She is searching for purpose.

She falls to the ground,
her face in her hands,
pulling her knees to her chest,
in a fetal pose of surrender.

A voice tells her to unfold,
to become a vessel,
to be filled
with possibility and purpose.

Lifted, no longer afraid,
she spreads her arms,
raises her face to heaven,
and breathes in the Spirit.

Debra Irsik

WHAT DO YOU WANT?

I want to receive the gift God
Has given me without reservation
I want to use my gifts
To become the person
I am meant to be
I want all fear of failure
Completely abolished
Wiped from my memory
I want to be strong
To stand up for my beliefs
No matter the cost
I want to find my true purpose
On this earth
In this moment
I want to feel that my life matters
That I have made a difference
For myself and generations to come

SNAPSHOTS

Every life changing moment
Every unnoticed moment
Is a snapshot of your story
The journey of life is a
Collection of snapshots
How you arrange
And
Develop them creates
Your personal story

LIFE

Like a river flowing
Gently lulling us into
Contentment
Complacency
Then storming in
Rushing
Ripping
Tearing away the calm
Awakening us to currents
That flood
Cleansing us
Forming us
Changing our direction
Carving fresh paths
An ever-changing
Adventure

NOT ENOUGH

Love is not enough on its own
Love opens the door
But
It does not grow
There are no results
In our lives–homes–communities
Or world
Without action

Action opens our minds to
Need
Need sparks the flame
To start a fire in our hearts
In the hearts of others
To identify the problems
Actively engage
Find a solution
Which creates a change

Debra Irsik

CREATURES OF HABIT

Don't like change
Schedules and lives
To rearrange
No surprises
I like my routine
Life laid out
Scene by scene

This virus is disrupting
With chaos and fear
Hoarding masses
Their purpose unclear
So ... just breathe
Let's take stock
Food
Water
Shelter
Check
Family safe
Now watch the clock

Wait for gestation
Let it run its course
We'll self-quarantine
Eliminate force
We're mostly good people
And we can tolerate change
We're creatures of habit
But we'll rearrange

We'll stand together
For family and friends
For community and country
Until the scourge ends

LOVE IS

Love was
A tsunami of passion,
Cresting, plummeting,
Sucking you into the deep,
Lifting you to start again.
Adrenaline rush.
Breathless kisses,
Electric touches.
Like the tides,
Ebb and flow,
So is love.
Mellowing, softening,
Need becomes us, not me.
Thoughts not I, but we.
A glance cherished,
A touch encouraged.
You, the other half of me.
We pant together at birth,
Cry together in death,
Pray together to reclaim faith.
Our beauty fades,
But I see in me
What you see,
The jewel that
Love is.

TRUE LOVE

Love means something different to me as I have grown older.
It evolves just like everything else in life.
I do not expect pounding hearts, breathless kisses,
or a passionate embrace.
It is so much more, an encouraging look, a supporting squeeze
of the hand
is as important as all of those things.
Knowing that someone supports me and believes in me is truly
love.
True Love is
Patient
Kind
Enduring, even in hard times.
Sharing respect for the gifts each is blessed with.
Supporting when life is battering.
Listening without judgement.
Ultimately, seeing your loved one
as God sees them, so it is ever changing.
Committed to the relationship
in Good times and in Bad.

Debra Irsik

WEDDED BLISS

You start the path as one
The road has just begun
The trial and tests are yet to come
Honey this is just the beginning

I don't cook like your mama cooks
I don't clean like your mama cleans
I don't care if you have a crease in your favorite jeans

You can eat peanut butter for days and days
But be sure to Say I Love You
In a million little ways

LOTS O' LAUGHS

Sometimes it ripples
from your head to your toes,
or maybe it trickles
and tickles your nose.

There's the hearty one
like Santa's Ho … Ho … Ho's;
The … I'm not sure one
that hiccups, stops and goes.

There are the high notes
that hit on your every nerve,
low gets my vote
swallowed, barely heard.

There is the shared laugh
that spreads around a room
in shimmering silver paths
til' every face is in bloom.

The laughter of the villain,
that evil snicker or sneer,
can leave you chillin'
unless a hero's near.

Gurgling laughs of children
can be innocent and true,
or … breathless and wild
if they're chasing you.

Debra Irsik

Laughter can lift spirits to soar,
turning gray skies to blue.
These giggling gifts
from me to you.

BLESSING QUILT

A blessing came my way today.
A patchwork trophy to display.
I did nothing to earn the gift,
but it gave my heart a welcome lift.

A gift given with no thought of return.
A selfless act from which to learn,
to share freely what we can.
No agenda or self-serving plan.

To see a need or feel a pull,
giving to others when life is full.
A touch, a coin, a simple word,
then the joy of giving is felt and heard.

Yes, a blessing came my way today,
A beautiful gift to display.
I'll find someone with a need,
pass on this joy and plant a seed.

Debra Irsik

SELF

Do you ever wonder
what happened to that
person of your youth?
That person filled with optimism,
excited about the discovery of tomorrow?

There is a fine line between
ego and self-worth.
Life has a way of
beating us down,
battering our confidence
telling us we're not good enough.

Do we always have a choice?
Or
Does circumstance dictate?
Can we break the cycle?
Was that person you dreamed of
a figment of your imagination?

The greatest tragedy of aging
is not the accumulation of years.
It is the loss of hope.
The idea of being stuck,
with no more adventures or discoveries.
The false idea that we no longer have purpose.

EMERGENCY

White lights with flashes of red
Great wings whirring
Fear
Waiting
Praying
A family gripped by uncertainty
Holding each other
Watching
Hearts in their hands

The beast hovers and lands
The loved one
Rushed to the gaping dragonfly
Whisked away
Dread and fear consume
Those who follow
They have no memory
Of the drive
No memory
Of the words spoken

Prayers pound in their heads
The dragon gives up her prey
The loved one will live another day
They breathe
This time

Debra Irsik

NOTES TO MY CHILDREN

1. If you hate me each time you are disciplined, you will hate me more than you love me.
2. I cannot fight your battles for you. You decide what is worth fighting for.
3. Do not stand your ground if it is crumbling beneath your feet.
4. Admit when you are wrong. Don't blame others for the consequences of your behavior.
5. My wish for you is that you will be a confident, caring and successful person, that you will be kind, generous and compassionate, with God at the center of your life.
6. I pray that when you stumble and fall from grace, you will find your way back to God.
7. Let go of the people that drag you under the current. They deserve your prayers, but not your life.
8. Don't let the shiny things of the world distract you. The genuine treasure is the love you share with others.
9. What matters is the purpose that each of us shares; to lead others into the grace and love of Christ by living our lives in a way that we can stand before Him and know we have a place in His kingdom.

TIME LET HER GROW
—*SESTINA*

Wasn't it yesterday? She was a child,
running around, jumping, laughing.
Somehow, time has stolen life.
Time has fast-forwarded to grow
this child into the person
standing before me that I love.

There is no greater love
than my aching for this child.
I recognize me in this person.
I can't help laughing;
I watched you grow
forgetting the tricks of life.

I am in awe of life,
captivated by total love.
I do not regret that I let you grow,
only that I miss the child.
The timber of her laughing
has changed. I see this person.

I see a woman in this person
with a vision of life.
And I am laughing
at myself, for I still love
this woman, my child,
that time let grow.
Time let her grow
into a beautiful person
with the heart of a child.

49

Debra Irsik

A woman that lives life,
with gentleness, kindness, and love.
She is strong, smiling, and laughing.

So infectious. Now I'm laughing.
In spite of me, you grow
stronger, becoming you. I love
This amazing person
Taking on life,
Fearlessly letting go of the child.

This beautiful person, full of life
and love that I watched grow.
This woman-child, that is now laughing.

JUST A BOY

The air is crisp, cold, clear.
Given a chance connection,
To turn us in a new direction.
Speeding down so near.

I watch his grace, his joy.
Wasn't it yesterday he started walking?
Not glaring and back-talking.
He's no longer a boy.

I lose myself in thought.
My son is growing into a man.
What happened to my plan?
I don't know why we fought.
I've been sweating the little things.
An orange flash goes speeding by.
My heart swells, I want to fly.
Let's see what tomorrow brings.

Suddenly I know,
God has brought us here.
To teach us to let go of fear.
So we can learn from this and grow.

I see my chance,

Debra Irsik

Setting my ski's straight down the slope.
I feel a flicker; a flame of hope.
There's surprise in his glance.

I smile and glide by.
My son is laughing.
This man I am passing.
Thank you, God, I sigh.

OUR SPECIAL FRIENDS

Their passion is real
every smile's sincere.
No agenda or intent
just open honesty.
This is their gift to each of us.
Pure trust, innocence, and love without condition.
You don't have to be beautiful or smart, tall, or thin.
Just you! How refreshing and inspiring.

They put their heart into everything they do.
Running with abandon around an old track,
with every ounce of energy they can muster.
Winning is not as important
as being there with friends.

They proudly wear their medals.
Sharing them at home, work, church,
and even the grocery store; with anyone
who smiles in their direction.
There are no strangers,
no difference is too great.
We are all equal in their eyes.

They are shunned, bullied,
mocked and sneered at.
Holding no grudge, they
forgive our transgressions,

Debra Irsik

with simple grace.
They run over the finish line
expecting a high five or hug,
wanting only our love,
and acceptance of their limitations.

If it is true that we are created
in God's image,
then surely those who:
Love simply,
laugh readily,
and smile, with their heart in their eyes
are the Portrait of God.
We call them many things: handicapped,
challenged, special needs, but maybe
we should add teacher to this list.
I think we can learn a lot from our special friends.

BEAUTY

Physical beauty is a gift to you
It will fade
Beauty of the soul
Is a gift to those around you
It will live on
In your spirit and
In all those you touch

TODAY

Today I will:
Love without thinking
Share without expectation
Smile spontaneously
Help with compassion
Pray with abandon
Believe with abundance
I will own my day
Today

Debra Irsik

RESPONSIBILITY

"No news is good news,"
or so it is said.
But we cannot ignore
what we've seen or read.

The world's in trouble.
There is more to come.
It can't be taken lightly.
There's nowhere to run.

Rivers barely flowing.
Air quality is poor.
Children are going hungry.
Dad's out the door.

With preservatives, cavities,
derivatives and additives,
"It's my life," teenage attitudes and
"I can fix it," political platitudes.

What It boils down to
I can clearly see,
each one of us must take
RESPONSIBILITY.

We are the ones to blame
for the mess we're in.
Not anyone or everyone
or your evil twin.

Give the bike a whirl.
Cut up the plastic.
You'll lose a pound or two.
Find your budget's elastic.

Can we make changes
in all this we own?
Can we take RESPONSIBILITY
for the seeds we've sown?

Debra Irsik

STICKS AND STONES

We can't take them back
We can sorrowfully chase them
Apologize and grovel
But once they are said
We can't take them back

We can forgive them
But not forget
They become a weapon
Arrows of anger and disappointment
Shooting spears at those we love

Soon their warmth cools
An open loving embrace
Becomes wary
The shard has planted itself
In their heart and they bleed

Again, we spew words
Without thinking about the consequences
We think we can take them back
But they stack up on one another
Soon there is an impenetrable wall
They look for criticism in every conversation
They find words of bitterness or jealousy
Creating an armor around their heart
Words can build up or tear down
Hurt or heal the ones you love
Choose them carefully

WHY CAN'T YOU SEE ME?

I am standing right here
you pass close enough to touch,
but to hope is too much,
because you can't see me.

Oh, you brush my sleeve
as you whisk by,
but you won't see me
only what you perceive me to be.

My skin is not pearly white.
My smile is overly bright.
My clothes, my shoes, my style
it's just … not right.

Why can't you see me?
The funny, fast, and fearless me;
not the fat, frumpy, or freaky me.
I want you to see the real me.

We are not so different.
We all want to be accepted.
Don't spurn me without cause,
Or ignore me without pause.

Can't you see

Debra Irsik

I am the shadow of you?
The you, who's afraid of rejection,
of not having group protection.

I am your fear.
You should see me
for who I am,
for truths on which I stand.

It's time to raise the bar.
Let each person be who they are,
the person they are intended to be.
Then you will see me.

FOOTPRINT

What is a carbon footprint?
Do we have one?
Is it cause for alarm?
Politico in a twitter
with Greta's effect.
What's the harm?

They cite fake news.
No global warming,
just radical environmentalist
swarming.
Ignore the signs.
Milk OSHA's gain.
We're doing fine.
There's no acid rain.

Yeah, oceans are dying,
coral reefs shrinking.
We have more earthquakes,
fires, and draught.
Pollution in water and air
fills our lungs,
but let's be fair.

We need fossil fuel
to move ahead.
Don't fill our minds
with doomsday dread.
Petroleum and coal
fuels our homes and our cars.

Debra Irsik

Wind energy impedes our view
of the stars.

So, continue to pump, frack, and strip
poor Mother Earth until she's sick.
Let the seismometers whir,
while we all gasp for clean air,
and follow our leaders
with that vacant stare.

Or

Initiate change,
you know.
Walk, don't ride.
Change the tide.
Adjust the stat.
Use less water please,
and if you need light,
use LEDs.

Don't waste food,
There's carbon there.
Eat local produce and share.
Recycle, repurpose, reuse.
If you travel, don't fly,
Take a cruise.

Turn off electronics.

It's not too hard.
Insulate better,
use Energy Star.
Choose not to be
a nation of sorrow.
Save our wildlife, our oceans, our children.
You know
save
TOMORROW!

Debra Irsik

"NOT" JUDGEMENT DAY

I awoke with a start, still in my bed.
All the images locked in my head.
Standing before Him,
the "Book of Life" in His hand.
He said, "It is not judgment day,
you will soon understand."

The Book open, my name carved inside.
He says, "Come closer. There is nothing to hide.
I know your shortcomings, your ins and your outs.
That is not what this day is about."

"It seems you are concerned with the judgment of others.
You scorn the sins of your sisters and brothers.
I bring you here to point out some facts.
To bring your attention to your own sinful acts."

"There was a man on the street and you looked down your nose.
He was hungry and lonely and wore tattered clothes.
I urged you to stop … or say a quick prayer,
but you kept right on walking as if he weren't there."

"A friend was in pain over her daughter's abortion.
You listened and prayed with her, but your mind was in mo-
tion.
(The girl is immoral, white trash, a lost cause.)
You added murder to the list without pause."

"Did you drop to your knees and send me a prayer?
Or think to say, Lord, are you there?
No, you raised her sin above all the rest.
In your mind, you list them, from the worst to the best."

"You seem to the world to be beyond reproach.
Your fashion, churchgoing, "Gucci" and "Coach."
I'll let you in on a little secret, my dear.
A sin is a sin, is a sin, Can You Hear?"

"I forgive you when you slander and blame,
break my laws, my commandments,
use my name in vain.
You're guilty of gossip, vanity, pride and worse.
You tell little white lies, you're a glutton, you curse."

"Now, before you judge the downtrodden drunk,
sort through the things in your very own trunk!
Only I can know what a heart truly holds,
If they might repent and reach lofty goals."

"Go back now, with your eyes open-wide.
Share my forgiveness; I'm by your side.
Your job is to listen, to pray, and send them home.
The Judgment rests here.
It is Mine alone."

Debra Irsik

EXCERPT FROM LIFE II
(From my journal, 2009)

I realize that I have spent my whole life doing what I think people want me to do. So, here I am, an older woman that doesn't have a clue who she is.

My daughter, Annie's, death haunts me. I question all that I believed. I feel that my faith has been based on the frailty of man. The truth comes from within us, not from what we read or are told. That is just the starting place in our journey.

I believe the Bible and other works of faith are still present today, because we need them as a foundation. We need something to make us think and question so we can find our truth. I do not believe there is a predestined plan for everyone. If He chooses us as great spiritual leaders, maybe He gives us a specific plan. I think God gives us tools to bumble around through life with until we discover the Holy Spirit. With the Spirit inside us, if we experience enough joy and pain in life, we find that voice.

I can sometimes only hear it softly but by serving others, and listening to the voice, it becomes stronger. Sometimes it is a struggle to recognize our blessings.

This section of Sunshine in the Weeds is a very condensed example of the process of my grief and healing after Annie's death. It is dark and sometimes seems hopeless, but life threw me lifelines in the weeds.

INTRODUCTION TO ANDREA NICOLE

This poem was written in 1981 in Annie's baby book. I asked Mike's niece, Michele, to read it at the wake. She later asked for a copy of the poem.

While struggling to make a copy come out the way I wanted it to, I highlighted the text and hit center. The poem came out in the shape of a tulip, Annie's favorite flower.

I believe this was one of many messages that Annie was safe in the arms of Jesus.

Many poems in this section of the book deal with faith and the questioning that plagued me after Annie's death. I hope following poem will bless you.

ANDREA NICOLE

It's such a pretty name.
Maybe it will bring fortune, or fame!
Of course, you may be more common,
but we'll love you just the same!
We may sometimes need reminded
that we are your caretakers for just
a time, and God has plans for your
life which are surely fine!
He has entrusted us with a beautiful
gift it's true, and we will do our very
best to love, nurture and care for you!
If all goes well, as I'm sure it will,
we will carefully help you grow.
The things of life both good and
bad, to you we will show.
Then one fine day you'll be a
woman so beautiful and kind and
some young man will take your hand, and
Oh! what a find!!
You'll leave our care and loving arms
only in words you know, for our hearts
will be with you forever and wherever
you go!

DEATH

Silently, stealthily, it creeps, like smoke, fog, or plague.
Claiming, innocence, youth, life.
No warning, no regret, or apology; just absolute darkness.
A light switched off.
The steady pumping of a heart … stops.
One last shallow breath, and a future is snuffed out.
No marriage or children or lover's embrace.
No laughter or songs or moments of grace.

What are we to make of life cut short?
Did God go, "Oops … let's abort?"

The memories to be made; mountains to climb;
world to explore … all gone.
In a moment, a whisper, it claims:
plans, hopes, and dreams,
of one loved, adored, and cherished.

A formidable foe, this thief called
"Death".

Debra Irsik

SATAN'S SPELL

With smoky, curling fingers,
it slips in and out.
Searching to plant a seed.
A tiny crevice left untended,
a place where fear sews
hopelessness and greed.

Patiently, he waits …
slithers into our minds.
Creating doubt that feeds.
Steadily it spreads and sends
tentacles into our spirit,
causing chaos and confusion.
You must take heed.

Cast out the world.
Close the gaps of
bad news and sludge.
Stand strong with the Creed.
The Holy Spirit
makes us whole.
Put your eyes on Jesus.
Let Him Lead.

ESCAPE

My mind wants to float away
Where it can't be found
Run from the tenacious
Howling hound

Silently read until I doze
Write of loves' red rose
Float on a cloud
Read out loud
With thunderheads, to hide me
Or
Be in a room full of puppies
Jumping and licking
Panting and kicking
Then
Float away again
Maybe take a nap
Without a care or map
No compass to guide me

Debra Irsik

FAÇADE

She smiles
She laughs
People see her in public
But they only see
What she wants them to see

They don't see
The shattered image in the mirror
That she sees
Each shard is an angry word
A slight or dig

A piece of the image
Becomes distorted
Perfection
Harmony
Bliss
Is mirage for their eyes
A façade

THE HEALING HEART

The human heart has an incredible
way of healing itself.
It will create a different path
for a blocked vein.

Our minds work much the same.
Faith is like our blood vessels,
the roadmap keeping
us on the path of life.

When life takes from us,
the heart must mend.
Just as blocked arteries
create a better route.

Sometimes that route is
less than it was.
Time seems held in a bubble.
You work:
Smile
Laugh
Cry
But it's surreal.

You are not fully present,
You are lost in a fog.
Time is your friend
you will mend,
but not forget.

Debra Irsik

FOG

Fog, that's where I am.
I see and feel
something on the edges.
I'm not sure I want to know
what is there.
Something lingers, but I'm weary,
too tired of the struggle.
It's easier to sit in the fog.

Let whatever is on the fringe
stay in the mist,
take care of itself.
If just today
I can stay
safely in the fog.
I don't engage,
question or doubt.
No passion, guilt, or pain.
Just stay in the mist.
Hide away
in the fog.

METAMORPHOSIS

Suddenly, that cocoon
that was both warm
and safe is smothering;
holding you down,
pinning you like a bug
on a board.
The warm blanket
is a straitjacket.
Fear holds you hostage.
You want to be a butterfly, but
What if you're a moth?

What if you don't have wings?

What if you have to crawl on the ground
and burrow into the earth?
What if you never find the purpose
for your life?

Should you just stay safe?
Wrapped up in that cocoon,
spinning around and around,
until you're spinning out of control.
What if you die there?
In the safety of the cocoon,
having never taken a chance.
Never breaking loose,
Never finding your wings or legs.
Never soaring or gliding,
floating or sailing or even

75

struggling.
What if you
are only
SAFE?
We cannot all be butterflies,
but … we can all achieve.
We can all soar and climb,
and in our own way.
We can all fly!

"Metamorphosis" was first published in The Write Bridge.

LIFE MOMENTS

Sometimes when we get weighed down,
we think life is about the struggle.
It's messy and ugly;
it is breathtaking and beautiful.
We need all these moments
to make it our best life.
Productive moments,
chaotic moments,
completely bombed moments.
We find ourselves
in these moments.
It's how we sink below the tide;
struggle to rise above,
and find ourselves
swimming again.
It's not whether we have
accumulated wealth,
found recognition or fame.
It is
having the satisfaction that:
We have walked our path,
Found our purpose,
Hard fought,
Hard won.

Debra Irsik

BRIDGES

We have bridges we cross as we travel,
and bridges to cross in our lives.
It is simply a tool to get across the chasms.
Sometimes wide and daunting, and
sometimes too wide to cross without support.

Our bridges come in many forms:
Friends who encourage and support us.
Life experiences that challenge and grow us.
Parents who guide and direct us.
Teachers who open our eyes and test us.
Religious teachers who lead us, opening our hearts
to the Spirit, that feeds us.
Jesus, who loves us;
Our bridge to
Eternal Life.

ONE

is not the loneliest number
The loneliest number is
Minus one
Losing one that is a piece of you
One that is
A piece of your heart
One
That is irreplaceable
A loss that never
Heals but leaves
An indelible scar

Debra Irsik

WHY MY CHILD?

Age makes no difference
to a mother.
Losing a child is like
losing a part of us,
whether they are newborn
or middle-aged.
A piece of us is gone.
We question the universe …
God.
We question ourselves,
Our purpose,
Our culpability,
Our existence.
Why my child?
Why when so many
seem to be less?
Less deserving of life.
Less deserving of love.
Less needed.
Why my child?

PAIN

Pain is the arrow
That pierces the soul
Pain is the anger you
Cannot let go
Pain is a part of our joys and sorrows
Pain is the reality of our tomorrows
There is no life
or love without pain
No sun or laughter
Without rain
So … Embrace it
It's what we know
Don't chase it
Eventually we grow

Debra Irsik

SORROW

Dank
Dark
Distant
Smothering
Smokey
Suffocating
Heavy waves of
       Sadness
       Overwhelming
       Raw
       Ragged
       Oppressive
       Wounds
Anger
Hate
Love
Tangled together in knots
Drowning in
Anguish and pain
Clawing at the fabric
We call life

TRICKSTER

He is slick and suave
Cool and cunning
Reels you in with
Charm and wit
Charisma like a magnet
People twitter about him
Like hummingbirds on jam
He convinces you he's needed
You are enthralled-hypnotized
The sacrificial lamb
You are faulty
Not whole - unworthy
You are nothing
You are less than nothing
You are
    Trapped
      Tainted
        Tricked
Into believing you need
The rush of worldly pleasure
The drug of greed
Don't sell your soul
He's the trickster
You see

Debra Irsik

SUNSHINE IN THE WEEDS

Bright translucent yellow petals
Wave to the weary traveler
Scattered in the ditches
Sunshine in the weeds

Sometimes sparse and spindly
Sometimes overtaking a hill
Peeking between the red cedars
Swaying on the edge of a field

These Kansas flowers of sunshine
Remind us that beauty flourishes in chaos
Clouds are temporary
Sunshine will come again

PART III:
SEASONS AND NATURE

Nature is Earth's heartbeat.

CACOPHONY IN THE QUIET

I wait in the car,
open my window,
a motor, a drill,
grasses swish swishing.

Wind whooshing, whispering.
A lawn mower hum.
A truck accelerating,
gravely changing of its gears.

A tractor backing on the street,
beep, beep, beep.
Birds singing their singular
tweet, tweet.

This … in the quiet.

It is over.
A bell rings,
car doors slam,
parents call hellos.

The quick patter
of children;
no methodical trudging.
Life awaits.

Another school day spent.

Debra Irsik

ANOTHER DAY

In the quiet misty morning
Peace
Whispering trees
Fountain trickles
Harmony for the dripping dew

Fawns stand watching
Ears twitch
Tail shudders alert
Clicking chattering squirrels

Day waking
Sun peeking
Ray's soft glow
Golden light rising
Slowly warming
Saturating
Nurturing
Street noise
Door opening
World awakes
Yet
Another day

SOUNDS

Consider sounds,
how they change or have different meanings.
Where does the sound of a train take you?
When you were a child,
did it mean adventure or travel,
saying goodbye?
Or was it a lonely sound?

Listen to life.
Clock's ticking.
Computers buzzing.
Phone's ringing, pinging.
Wind stirring and rising.
Birds singing and cooing.
Squirrels chattering.
The bawling calf and lowing cow.
Traffic noise.
Pebbles crunching, twigs snapping underfoot.
A baby crying or laughing,
the squeal of a happy child.
Water dripping, trickling, sloshing.
Scraping of a shovel or rake.
The tinkle of a bell.
Hammer against metal.
The creak of a door.
The flutter of wings against your window,
or

Debra Irsik

Night sounds?
The owl inquiring,
coyote howling,
cat's caterwauling.
Crickets and cicadas playing
their symphonies.
Frogs croak in harmony.
The moon and stars
silently watching.

MOODS OF THE SKY

Soft billowy clouds float
on a canvas of blue.
We make a game of
telling what we see:
A galloping horse,
roaring tiger,
unicorn.

Sometimes it's a peaceful sky
changing as we sleep.
Becoming a
weeping, rumbling, groaning
churning, angry canopy,
exploding with fireworks,
illuminating the heavens.
Then shaking the earth with wind,
sheets of chilling rain, ice, snow.

Illusions of geological layers.
Hard gray stone,
that rolls and churns
twisting into ropes of disaster.
Tearing through
towns and limestone hills.
Throwing trees and poles
like an angry child,
with no distinction of value.
No mercy.

Sometimes it's a sheet of the bluest blue
with a hesitating dot and dash,

like a secret code.
A hint of breeze, hot, dry.
Or
thick, dark gray,
no white in sight.
A brisk wind stirs
the poplars to applaud, and
their leafy cousins, to dance.

So many faces of the
Passionate,
Peaceful,
Overwhelming,
Glorious,
Moods of the sky.

THUNDER SHOWER

Running out, the door swinging behind,
"it's sprinkling," they chime.
Standing with their arms stretched out,
"catch the rain," they shout!
Lifting little faces up
lapping drops, no cup.
Dancing in the rain, they smile,
marching through puddles single file.
Authentic joy,
each girl and boy,
Raindrops glistening in their hair.
Smiles are contagious there.
Just a shower here and gone,
they're not sad, not one.
Now there's mud to entertain,
no more thoughts of summer rain.
Their clothes mud-caked,
little faces brown and baked.
Sun comes out to touch each flower.
Now, time for an actual shower!

WATER

River's fill
    From the hills,
        From the mountains
            Blessed with rain.
Reservoirs overflow.
    Spill into thirsty streams
        Flowing into rivers,
            Winding, trickling, rushing.
              They find their way,
To the sea.
    Pulsing with rhythm
      In perfect time with earth and sky.
        It's ebb and tides in tune,
With wind and endless time.
The time set by God with seasons change.
Man develops and encroaches on beaches.
He sucks the black gold from beneath her.
            Still, she keeps her rhythm even with the tumult,
              Of hurricane or tsunami, her deep pulse remains.
              The heartbeat of advancing and retreating.

CHANGE

The morning air is crisp,
apples and pumpkins abound.
Leaves turn shades of yellow and red,
brightening our world before they shed.

Trees prepare for winter's sleep.
Storing energy
grasses and flowers do the same,
playing Mother Nature's game.

We bundle up for brisk walks,
through neighborhoods and parks.
Leaves crunch beneath our feet
the scent of Fall both sharp and sweet.

Hoarding Winter's cache,
burying their treasure,
squirrels hustle with cheeks full.
Animals grow coats of wool.

We too must prepare.
Life is like this ancient cycle.
Coming and going, we rearrange.
Like the seasons, we must change.

WIND SONG

Whispering secrets heard as she passes through the trees.
Fluttering, shaking, caressing, thousands of shimmering leaves
Cooling the farmer's brow, whipping up dust devils in the fields,
Bringing the promising scent of rain and hope of better yields.
Blowing the sail full, bringing a catamaran to rest,
lifting the hem of a young girl's dress.
Flag gently waving with a breath of air,
or billowing wildly with a gust and fanfare.
Dancing on the pavement, leaves crisp and brown,
swirling high in the air, slowly spiraling down.
Holding the magic of a train's lonesome note,
cherishing a memory as the melody floats.
Oh! the fury of the hurricane gale,
or spinning and churning–as tornado spits hail.
She soothes us … cools us, her repertoire has no end,
this blustering, billowing, breezy thing called simply … wind

AUTUMN

The colors are of earth, not sky
No soft pinks or blues
Dusty rusted tired
Somber earthy hues
Of orange brown red
With golden highlights
Spun around her head

These are the colors
That remain
Rushing through
The grasses veins
Trees naked and gray
Celebrating
      Surviving
          Resting
Dormant on this day

They wear these colors
Then they sleep
Jubilant and proud
Their parade will keep
Until the bloom of Spring
When all awake
To hear the robins sing

SNOW

White
soft
quiet
A blank canvas waiting for life to
change it
paint it
imprint the motion of creatures and man.
Snow
silent
glistening
bright.
A squirrel dances gingerly under the
tutu of an oak with a barren top.
The cat shakes her paw.
wonders at the feel of
Snow
cold
wet
intricate.
A single flake, unique design
no other can duplicate.
Like a finger print
not one the same.
Snow
amazing
beautiful
gracefully falling,
created by God.
Snow

WINTER CLOUDS

Barren boney-fingered trees
Reach to the heavens
Searching for
Life in winter clouds
Brooding dark filtering light
Holding back the warmth of the sun,
Teasing
With glorious sunrises
Sunsets that dazzle
Waiting for the melting
Season
Heavy with snow or icy rain
Turning the boney fingers
Into a crystal wonderland
Sometimes
Dumping random mounds
Of white, Cossack hats
Accents to counter
Starkness
Winter clouds the canopy
In nature's rhythm
A time to gather strength
Storing nourishment preparing
Sun
Breaks through the gray quilt
And warms the earth
A peek at the fluff of white
Soon

Debra Irsik

Light will come with
The thunderheads of
Spring
And
Summer skies

WINTER

Winter's cold
Dreary days
Long nights
Seeking sun
Heat on face
Icy wind
Chill to bone
Dry eyes and skin
Ice
Snow
Frost
Beautiful curse
Paradox
Mesmerizing beauty
Crystal world
Mirage
Glacial danger
Frigid walks
Treacherous road
Hostile friend
Temporary
With
First bud

Debra Irsik

WISH FOR MAY
—SONNET

I know I wished for spring to come today
But snow weighs heavy on the buds and leaves
No sun but now white fluff in which to play
Which bends each stately plume down to its knees

Snowy visage just doesn't seem quite right
I scuff my toe into the sugar stuff
Those soft curves piled high with glistening white
Plunging my fists down deeper in my muff.

My gaze takes in the sparkling crystal world
It seems a shame to wish the day away
I raise my hands spinning until I'm furled
down upon the shimmering snow I lay

I will resign to change my wish for May
Snow angels fly and play the day away

THE SYMPHONY OF SILENCE

Trees glisten with new fallen snow.
Wind gusts, rustling leaves.
I hear whispers;
The snap of a twig,
Song of a cardinal,
Swish of my skis as I bump along.
The orchestration of nature rises and
Falls in the shadows of the trees.
A heated twittering from a thicket,
Scolding me for my intrusion.
A chattering squirrel bounds effortlessly,
Soundlessly across the snow.
The birds are forgiving of my blunder,
Chirping and singing their parts
With no obvious rhythm or rhyme.
Wind adds a shudder … a flutter
And retreats, holding its breath,
Only to inflect again more intensely,
Making slender trees creak and sway.
Adding natural notes to the harmony.
This masterpiece,
This symphony of silence.

SPRING

Trees burst with color, no longer barren.
Crocus, jonquils, then tulips bloom to add color to the canvas.
Squirrels scurry about and birds sing, "It's spring, it's spring."

Spring brings the promise of new life and renewal.
All that was dormant springs to life.
Hope seems to come to life as well.
How suitable that we celebrate Easter in this season.
Everything that seems dead rises to life.
We give Glory to the awesomeness of God.

These times seem very troubled with natural disasters:
wild-fires, tornadoes, hurricanes, wars, and unrest.
We wonder if this is the time.
Spring reminds us that even after death, there is life.
We have hope of a brighter tomorrow.
We have the promise of life eternal.

BIG FLAT MOON

One dimension
On twilight sky
A white marble sticker
on the eastern horizon.
The blush of pinks and oranges
wane in the west.

Are the coyotes that
howl at the sticker moon
flat like Flat Stanley?
Are they known as,
Flat Coyote?

Where is the depth of this disc?
How does it hide its edges?
If we were looking down
from this moon would we
look like paper-dolls
in a one-dimension world?
Would we get thick and round,
as the moon rose higher?

PART IV:
FAITH AND HOLIDAYS

The cross is our foundation. Our arrow, our direction.

NEW BEGINNING

In the beginning, God created earth,
and set it spinning in the universe.
He paused and saw that it was good,
so He adorned it with mountains and woods.

He formed a man in His image from clay,
teaching him to work, worship, and pray.
God could create true perfection, but
man was to choose his own direction.

Alas, man was stubborn, choosing to sin.
God, in His great mercy, forgave again and again.
He was endlessly patient, His chastisement firm,
but in ignorance, man refused to learn.

"I need a Shepard to gather this flock,
I'll send my own Son, to lead and take stock."

Christ's birth was another beginning, but
His life was required for man's sinning.
God did not leave us standing alone
though Jesus had risen to Heaven's throne.
The Holy Spirit descended to fill every heart
and when called upon, He will not depart.

In the beginning, our God, wholly one,
now a triune God is leading us on.
New beginnings through sorrow's strife,
brings the Glory of God, and Everlasting Life.

Debra Irsik

HOLY SPIRIT

You won't feel different
no blinding light
But He is there
just not in sight

Deep inside you
when you need Him most
The flame ignites
you become the host

Nurture this gift
call upon the Spirit
His voice is there
Listen … you will hear it

THE HAND OF GOD

When you see the beauty of an iris or rose;
the intricate details of the universe,
our galaxy and stars.
Or watch a flock of birds, swooping
in unison, to form a pattern
up, down, and around.
Forming a perfect circle,
then breaking away
into another beautiful movement
of their majestic ballet.

To think that this creature could
just happen, to have a sensitivity
to the winging of the bird beside them;
an innate sort of GPS.
No explanation makes sense,
except the hand of God.

CROSSES

Have you ever noticed
that crosses are everywhere?
Support in construction
of our homes and buildings.
The transmission of our voices,
electric veins that stand along our roads
and fields.
Rows and rows of crosses.
We cross our fingers for luck
or protecting the truth.
Every intersection in life forms a cross.
We use it in cross-stitching,
basket weaving,
braiding ... plumbing ... math.
Our radio towers,
radar devices,
even birds flying by
look like crosses in the sky.
Stick people even resemble the cross.
We have cross-bows,
cross hatching ... cross latching,
We get cross-wise.
Don't forget to cross your t's.
The arrow that gives
direction is a form of a cross.
It is simple to see that the Cross
Is our foundation
Our arrow
Our Direction.

HE IS IN THE SHADOWS

Standing in the shadows
You may not know He's there,
But He will light the darkness
Follow you with care.

Calming stormy seas
When others abandon you,
He will steer the vessel.
He will see you through.

He'll share your joy and sorrow,
Lift your burdens, bear your load.
Stand with you in the fire,
And when your story's told;

He will guide you on the journey,
Take your hand in his own
Through the gates of heaven
He will take you home.

Debra Irsik

THE SAVIOR'S BIRTH

Bells are ringing,
Choirs singing,
Tidings of good cheer.

People rushing,
Fixing stuffing;
But why are we here?

A babe, they're saying,
Singing, praying,
Bethlehem, we hear.

Stop the rushing;
Forget the stuffing.
Truth is strong and clear.

We're forgetting;
That long ago setting.
The Savior's birth draws near.

GREATEST GIFT

A Shining Star
does not waiver;
Holds steady for
kings to come.
Not yet born this
storied Savior,
The Blessed Promised One

Three Wise men
from Orient lands,
travel to welcome
a King.
Foretold by prophets;
so by faith
precious gifts they bring.

Would we believe?
Would I follow that star,
in this world of doubt and fear?
Would we have thought it strange,
and scoffed at what we now
hold dear?

LOST VALENTINE

Wandering slowly through the store
inhaling the aged smell.
Antique furniture, coins, and more.
A unique mix to sell.

I hoped to find a treasure.
I could feel impending glory.
Little did I know the measure
of the unfolding story.

I meandered toward the back,
where my heart did truly lie.
Forgotten books, haphazard stack.
I caressed one with a sigh.

A valentine, yellow with age,
fell from an ancient text.
I gently turned the fragile page.
Pure magic happened next.

Cupid's arrows mark is true,
for printed there in rhyme,
were heartfelt words of love so new,
which took me back in time.

My dearest Jane,

I leave within the week for a sojourn across the sea,
I can only hope that you will wait for me.
My heart is in your hands if only you'll be mine
Please be my Valentine!

I fear I tarried far too long.
My words are too abrupt and strong.
Alas, there is no time to waste,
My darling Jane, I must make haste.

You will be lonely, never alone,
For my heart remains there with your own.
Will you wait for me and share my life?
I am asking you to be my wife.

Cupid's laugh is gleefully pealing
from the Heavens far above.
What is this euphoric feeling?
Dear God ... so this is love!

Marry Me
Love forever,
Joe

Debra Irsik

ASHES TO ASHES

Dust to dust

This season

Reflection
Repentance
Remembrance
Rejoicing
Resurrection

Reflect on your life
Repent your shortcomings
Remember Christ's forty-days
Rejoice in the promise
Resurrection
Victory over death
No fear
No suffering
His perfect gift
Eternal life

BLESSED MOTHER

Blessed Mother, you answered the call.
Holy Mother of Jesus and of us all.
It must have been hard to watch him grow to a man,
Knowing that He was the sacrificial lamb.

Did you call out to God to change the plan of salvation
To save your son over all creation?
I feel your pain, your anguish and tears,
The times you wanted to hide from your fears.

To steal Him away, protect Him from fate.
Begging the Father to let him escape,
But deep in your heart, you stayed true and strong
You knew to obey, to resist would be wrong.

Knowing from the start, His destiny set in stone,
You raised Him and loved Him. He was not truly your own.
We honor you, Holy Mother of God.
We thank you for this rocky path you've trod.

I pray to persevere in the trials I face,
To use the model of your love and grace.

Debra Irsik

WHAT IF?

all we've learned
about death, God and resurrection,
the last question,
the answer we all seek.
What if it's not true?
What if there is only this?
No afterlife … only returning to dust.
What if they got it wrong?
What if death is forever, and
Christ's resurrection is a giant hoax?
What if Jesus was a fraud?
What if there is no hope, no God?
What if your existence is zero to ninety,
with no chance of redemption?
The bigger question is,
What if they are right?

HERO'S REWARD

A warrior wears his battle scars
with pride upon his face.
Across his breast a row of stars,
he brings us no disgrace.

He's welcomed with a big parade,
'Hero' they proclaim;
but in his heart, the whole charade
pounds within his brain.

The memories haunt his every dream
no sleep is ever content.
Faces; women and children scream
the weapon's round is spent.

Each life is counted on this earth.
We hold all children dear.
Somewhere she who gave him birth,
shall never hold him near.

The terrors implode, consume his life.
He cannot live with this heavy yoke;
no friends, no job, or wife.
He's hungry, lonely and broke.

"It's a disorder, some big name,
send him to a shrink."
There has to be something to blame,
but it's not what one would think.

He is not weak or just depressed.
His demon's drive him mad!
Another 'Hero' put to the test,
we say, "It's just too bad."

Debra Irsik

"OLD GLORY"

That flag we call "Old Glory"
Stands for Freedom hard won
One Nation under God
Our pledge to Native sons
Those bold stripes painted
With blood of soldiers
Young and old
Courage bolstered by prayers
And His holy word
Our founders built this nation
With God as our foundation
We believe their hearts were true
Their courage and God's grace
Will see us through

PART V:
OUR WORLD

Every breathtaking moment is a testament to Him.

WHO SAID?

Who said Kansas is flat?
The Flint Hills beg to differ.
They flow with seas of
Native grasses from
Marshall county in the north
To Cowley in the south.

Take a drive through
Endless green and rolling hills;
Cattle peppered here and there,
Often with suckling calves,
Standing on a limestone shelf.

Layered rock, intricate veins
Weaving a tale
Or pebbles on the hilltops
As if Goliath dropped his bag of
Stones for his slingshot.

Stepping stones for the ages
Along streams and pools.
History embeds its stories
Of wandering tribes, and
Wondrous adventure.

Debra Irsik

NEW ROUTE

Hay … rolls and rolls
Of fresh baled hay
Cornfields
Dried and brown
Ready for the
Giant green jaws
Sunflowers bowed heads
Their zenith gone
Fruit ready for harvest

Concrete dinosaurs
Dot the horizon
Silver mammoths
Hold the bounty
Until grain cars
Lined like soldiers
Await hungrily

Barren wheatfields
Seed soon ground
Bags of flour
Begging luscious concoctions
Of golden bread
Cinnamon wafting
In sticky daydreams
Deserted farmsteads
Roofs collapsed burying
Lost memories of
Past inhabitants
Red cedar invades
Pastures without notice

While cattle graze
Chewing their cud

Serpentine aluminum and steel
Spout water into
The atmosphere
Ignoring new technology
With the age-old adage,
If it's not broken
Don't fix it

Seeing Kansas
With eyes in the past,
Settled in sameness
Like time stopped
Still getting by
In slow motion

Published in Writing From the Center, Vol. 1, Kansas, 2023.

Debra Irsik

THE LION

Sad and striking
This carving in honor of
Swiss guards who
Gave their lives
For a country not their own
Bravery
Honor
Service
The lion represents
All
Who gave all
For freedom and prosperity
So, generations to come
Will remember
War has no winners

ROME

Ancient stones, their secrets keep.
Peter whispers from marble lips.
Beneath them, saints and sinners' sleep.
A master's creation from his fingertips.

The life and death of Christ;
Carved cathedral door.
Weary travelers learn
Though no common tongue,
Hope born of resurrection
From a life of sacrifice.

Wealth, corruption, brutality,
History held captive, gone.
Proof of the reality,
Truth depicted in stone.

ADELBODEN

The landscape changes
Foothills
Dotted with Charolais
Wheat
Fields of oats
And round bales of hay

Villages close together
Stone houses with worn red roofs
Farms laid out in squares
And meadows divided by hedges
No fences

We arrive in our village
Neatly arranged with a
Grocery
Pharmacy
Sandwich shop
Pristine streets
No trash

Views that
Suck the air from
Your lungs
Transporting you
Into a picture postcard

CENTRAL PARK

They said no rain 'til 3:00
It is not yet 11:00
Water drips off my nose
My eyelashes leave
Black streaks
Punctuation
under my eyes

My hair leaks cold
Down my uncovered neck
Wave ...
Whistle ...
A yellow cab streaks by
Full of dry passengers

I brought an umbrella
It is dry
In my bag
At the hotel
They said no rain 'til 3:00

Debra Irsik

STATELY STATUE

Hot wind blows our hair back.
We watch the mountains of brick towers
Become a cityscape on a canvas of blue.

The wake behind the ferry is
a testament to the motion away.
She stands serene as we approach.
The Manhattan bridge is a web
for the people-ants that weave across.

She holds her torch high
to guide the weary, travel worn,
displaced souls of the world
to a better tomorrow.

Staunch and solid,
a promise to the masses.
Remember:
Grandfathers, grandmothers,
Mothers, fathers, friends,
Immigrants all.

FLORENCE

A picturesque villa
Overlooking olive groves in quilted rows
Vineyards already harvested
Sunflowers a bright contrast

Stately whitewashed stucco walls
Red slated roofs
Beaded entries
Time worn furniture
Dancing on terracotta floors

Paths tiled with
Tuscan shades
Umber … sienna … ochre
The earthen colors
Olde world

I will dream of this place
Tucked amid ancient cities
Of hot quiet nights
A place of thought
And story

LAND OF THE ALPS

Breathtaking beauty
Trees so dense the mountains
Seem to be covered in velvet moss
Clouds hang over the highlands
Keeping the highest peaks in shadow
A meadow is slipped between
The rolling rounds
Cows graze and low
The tinkling of a bell
Floats on a breath
Of mountain air
The whisper of trees
With stories to tell
Calls for solitude
Introspection
Peace
Silence
Soft whishing of a waterfall
Trilling of a bird
Enveloped in a world
Depths unexplored

SWISS HAVEN

We step back in time
Green slopes peppered with cows
A tinkle of a bell teases you
It's as if Heidi might be
Right around the corner

Everywhere your gaze pauses
There is a new page for a calendar
A picture postcard 360 degrees
Waterfalls cascading soundlessly
Down velvet slopes
Men shirtless swinging scythes
And raking hay into small
Pyramids to be picked up
With a bailer from a bygone era

A precarious ladder
Of stone and earth
Leads to a reflective
Pool at the bottom of
A mountain waterfall
Where we cool our feet
In this ancient haven

Debra Irsik

DREAM OF BEACHES

Hot cloudless days
Warm nights
Shifting glances
Observing cultures
Other than ours
With bright, summer colors
Umbrella drinks abound

Billowing fabrics
For tropical climates
Markets crowded
With tourist items
To take a little beach
Back home

The sand is warm
Sugary soft
Sticks to your feet
Little fish
Chase your bright suit
Nibbling and darting

Fish and sea life
Flourish in the
Transparent crystallin sea
Swimming in schools
Synchronized ballets
Like birds in a flock

The evening cools
The ferry floats

On a sheet of foaming glass
Sun sits on the water
A reflection of fire
Rippling like a mirage
In your dream
Of beaches

Debra Irsik

SOUTHERN COMFORT

Ocean Breeze
Winding roads
Green wall of trees

We snake though
Missouri-Kentucky-Tennessee
Find Charleston waiting
Patiently

Ocean surf
Sun and green
Aging wooden jetties
Gulls suspend ... dive and preen

Catching my breath
I walk on the beach
Wind in my hair
Horizon in my reach

PART VI:
WORDS AND WRITING

Writers must write

WORDS

Words swim in my head.
Thoughts float in and out,
or speed by bouncing
like errant bubbles,
off the corners of my mind,
crashing into each other,
bursting into droplets,
splashing with no form
onto the flat blank nothing.

Stringing together the letters;
I try to make a single word.
They scramble even as I
line them up,
rutht, driefn, rutst.
No meaning until they
have structure and form.
Truth, friend, trust,
strong words that are nothing
without order.

Without structure
we are nothing,
garbled like the words.
Until we find form, structure,
and purpose.

Debra Irsik

WRITING RHYTHM

Pit-a-pat
Tap-tap-tap
Pit-a-pata tappity tap
Words falling
Around me
Like rain patter
Making my keyboard
Clickety clack tap-tap-tap
Tappity tap clack-clack
Splatter on the page
Words raining down
I try to catch them in my mind
With my hands, my heart
Too fast
They rain down

WRITING SPARK

Spark is a beginning.
The tiny glow,
that ignites the fire
within every writer.

It is the little thing
in the heart of every writer
that drives us to put pen
to paper telling our stories.

We have the potential to
start a fire or calm a storm.
When we share our words,
we can fuel imaginations.

We can build worlds,
mend hearts and minds,
connect to history, and
share our love
of the written word
with the world.

Debra Irsik

WRITING HEROES

Writers are brave.
revealing themselves, vulnerable and naked.
Willing to allow the world to see them
with their essence and flaws.

When a writer writes,
they expose their inner-most thoughts.
Feelings laid bare, inviting
criticism, chastisement, scorn.

Their writing may also
invite accolades, love
or encourage others to share stories.
They touch lives, connecting others.

Writers are heroes with the pen as their sword.
They open minds and hearts,
inciting laughter, tears, joy, pain, and imagination.
Revealing injustice, culture, and creation.

In this world of chaos,
writers build kingdoms and worlds.
Their worlds sweep away cares
taking us on magical journeys.

Writers paint pictures
in poetry, prose and verse.
Delighting the tongue, enriching
our past present and future.

ABOUT THE AUTHOR

Deb Irsik is a Kansas girl and shares her life with her husband Mike and children, John and Emily. She is a member of The Kansas Authors Club and Emporia Writing Group.

Deb completed her three book, Middle-grade fiction series, Heroes by Design, in 2020. She has dedicated her time to writing essays, prose and fiction, and completing this collection of poetry. She has been published in 105 Meadowlark Reader, The Write Bridge, and Writing from the Center.

Deb can be found online at:

www.facebook.com/D.A.IrsikAuthor
Web: www.dairsik.com

Milton Keynes UK
Ingram Content Group UK Ltd.
UKHW052126070624
443665UK00007B/141/J